THE SCHOOL
John Burningham

Jonathan Cape Thirty Bedford Square London

When I go to school

I learn to read

And to write

Sing songs

Eat my dinner

Paint pictures

Play games

Make friends

And then go home

Little Books
by John Burningham

THE BABY

THE RABBIT

THE SCHOOL

THE SNOW

THE DOG

THE BLANKET

THE FRIEND

THE CUPBOARD